लव फॉर्म डिस्टैंस

मुस्कान सचदेव

Copyright © Muskan Sachdeva
All Rights Reserved.

क्रम-सूची

क्रम-सूची

क्रम-सूची

क्रम-सूची

प्रस्तावना

लॉन्ग डिस्टेंस रिलेशनशिप अक्सर बहुत ही मुश्किल और नामुमकिन मने जाते हैं. पर वो एक सचाई हैं. जिनसे आप प्यार करते हैं उनसे दूर रहना आपके प्यार की सबसे कठिन परीक्षा है जो आपके रिलेशन को सबसे ज़्यादा मजबूत बनती है. इस पुस्तक में 45 लोगों ने लॉन्ग डिस्टेंस रिलेशन पर अपनी भावनाए प्रस्तुत की हैं.

पावती (स्वीकृति)

मई सबसे पहले भगवन को धन्यवाद करना कहती हूँ की उन्होंने ने मेरा हर वक़्त साथ दिया.

मई अपने माता पिता को भी धन्यवाद् देना कहती हूँ की उन्हें मुझपे पूरा विश्वास है.

मई उसन सभी लोगों को धन्यवाद् देना कहती हूँ जो इस पुस्तक में मेरे साथ थे और साथ ही साथ पोएटिक सोल्स के फाउंडर "रोहन नाथ" का भी बहुत सुक्रिया.

पोएटिक सोल्स की पूरी टीम को बहुत बहुत धन्यवाद् मेरी इस बुक को परफेक्ट बनाने के लिए.

Lovers From Far By Compiler Muskan Sachdeva

People always said to me long distance love never works. How can you trust someone blindly from this distance? How do you know that the person on the other side of phone is true and genuine? How can share your dark secrets with someone you haven't met ever? How can you share your love with someone you haven't even seen?

To all those people who have these questions in their mind, here is my reply to these questions!!!!

Yes you can trust someone who is on the other side of the phone. When someone cares for you, shows your their love, share your happiness as well as your sorrows then they are someone you can trust blindly. When someone on the other side of phone is listening to all your dark secrets and promising to keep them safe then that person is genuine. When that person is also sharing their secrets with you without thinking will you keep them safe or not then that person is true spirit.

Love is distance is hard but not impossible. But when you are far from that person you both get to know each others real value real importance in your life. And the value that person holds in your life gives you hope and spirit to be with that person forever and not break the bond.

Love distance relationship are hard but it's the best bond ever because both fall in deepest love for each other. It's the best bond because no one uses the other for anything they remain far and carve to see each other. It's best bond because when you see each after years you can't wait to see each other and the love grows and grows and grows.

About The Compiler

This is Muskan Sachdeva. She hails from Basti Uttar Pradesh. She is presently pursuing her masters. She loves writing and has been co authored in more than 70 anthologies. This book is her second compilation.

1
Aastha Singh

Aastha Singh, a 19, she resides in Lucknow and pursuing B.A. She believes that she can bring her thoughts, experiences and feelings through writing. Her hobbies are writing, listening music, dance and traveling.

"इंतज़ार"

"दीदी, देखो ये क्या हो रहा है? रेगुलेटर ऑन ही नहीं हो रहा है।" सिया ने चिल्लाते हुए कहा। "रुको" कहते हुए रजत ने रेगुलेटर सही से लगाया और ऑन कर दिया।

दोनों ने एक-दूसरे को देखकर प्यारी-सी स्माइल की। फिर रजत बाहर चला गया और सिया किचन में ही चाय बनाने लगी।

रजत और सिया एक-दूसरे को बचपन से जानते थे। बचपन में दोनों साथ खेले, लड़ाई भी की और एक दूसरे की पिटाई भी। लेकिन उनकी मुलाकात कभी-कभी ही होती थी, जब उनकी छुट्टियाँ होती और वो एक दूसरे के घर जाते।

दरअसल दोनों के परिवारों में अच्छी बैठक थी और एक परिवार की तरह प्यार था उनमें। इसलिए दोनों का मिलना हो ही जाता था, पर कभी-कभी। इस बार भी दोनों की मुलाकात इसी तरह हुई, पर काफी दिनों बाद।

अब दोनों बच्चे नहीं थे, बड़े हो गए थे। अब वो लड़ाइयाँ या खेल नहीं होते थे। अब तो दोनों ज्यादा बातें भी नहीं करते थे, शायद अब दोनों शर्मीले हो गए थे ये थी इसकी वज़ह। लेकिन भले ही वे होंठों से बात नहीं करते थे पर उनकी आँखे सब कुछ कह देती थी। वैसे तो बचपन में दोनों कई बार मिले, लेकिन इस बार कुछ तो अलग था।...आखिर क्या था? ये तो सिया और रजत को भी समझ नहीं आ रहा था।

रजत को देखते ही सिया के चेहरे पर मुस्कान आ जाती लेकिन वो चाहकर भी रजत से बात नहीं कर पाती।

आखिर क्यों...? ये तो सिया की समझ से बाहर था।

उधर रजत का हाल भी कुछ ऐसा ही था।

बस दोनों का एक शौक़ दोनों को करीब आने का मौका जरूर देता था, वो था- क्रिकेट।

"सिया! ऐसे बॉलिंग करोगी तो शशांक कभी आउट ही नहीं होगा।"

रजत ने सिया को चिढ़ाते हुए कहा।

"अच्छा, तो लो तुम ही कराओ बॉलिंग और एक ही बॉल में सबको ऑउट कर देना।" इतना कहकर सिया बॉल फेंकते हुए चली गई।

"अरे, मैं तो मज़ाक कर रहा था।" कहते हुए रजत भी उसको मनाने चल दिया।

दिन ऐसे ही बीतते गए। लेकिन दोनों में ज्यादा बात नहीं हुई।

कल रजत को वापस जाना था। वो मौका ढूँढ़ रहा था सिया से बात करने का। पर सिया को तो जैसे उसके जाने से कोई फर्क़ ही नहीं पड़ रहा था या फिर वह ये दिखाना ही नहीं चाहती थी कि उसे कोई फर्क़ पड़ता है।

"मैं कल जा रहा हूँ।" मौका मिलते ही रजत ने सिया से कहा।

"अच्छा" सिया ने सिर हिलाते हुए कहा।

"घर चलोगी मेरे साथ?" रजत ने पूछा

"नहीं ..." इतना कहकर सिया मुस्कराते हुए कमरे से बाहर चली गई।

अगले दिन...

रजत चला गया। बस जाते-जाते सिया से इतना ही कहा- "जाने का मन नहीं हो रहा है।" सिया ने फिर भी कुछ नहीं कहा।

दोनों भले ही दूर हो रहे थे, पर उनका मन तो अभी भी एक-दूसरे के पास ही था।

अब दोनों के पास कुछ था तो बस कुछ खूबसूरत यादें और दोबारा मिलने का इंतजार...।

2
Ajay Verma

I'm Ajay Verma 21 year old aspiring writer, I believe in the writing in form of love, and motivation as poetry and stories. I love to travel and explore new thoughts about any field

By profession I'm a pharmacist .
And my hobbies are writing poetry , quotes , story etc.

तुम और मैं इस प्यार मैं

आज मैंने पूछा उस ख़ुदा से दो पल की जो यह ज़िंदगी है।

वक्त के साथ सब बदलता है। आज बचपन है तो एक रोज़ जवानी है।

ओर ज़िन्दगी के गुज़रते हर पड़ाव पर एक रोज़ ख़त्म होने वाली जो
मेरी ये कहानी है।

चाहत तो मेरी आज भी कुछ ओर है ओर मुझे मिला कुछ ओर है।

रास्ते अलग है सफ़र एक रोज़ आपस मै मिलजाना है।

वो तो मेरी रूह ने मुझे सम्भाला है ।

क्योंकि मुझे मेरा कल जो गवारा है।

काश मेरी हर किताब मै ज़िक्र हो तेरा हर जुबा पर नाम हो तेरा इतनी
सी तेरी कहानी है।

जब उन किताब के फटे पन्नों के जेसे हवा मै बिखर रही थी ज़िंदगी जो
मेरी

काश वापिस वो जुड़ जाये।

एक उम्मीद की तरह टूटे थे जो सपने मेरे एक बार फिर वो उस आसमाँ
मै

सज।

जाये कुछ पलों की बची मेरी ज़िंदगानी एक बार वापिस मुस्कुरा जाए।

मेरी यह दुआ है उस ख़ुदा से जब हो जाऊँ मै मुक्कमल एक वक्त पर
तो साथ हो तुम।

रह जाए कुछ अधूरे सपने जो साथ देखे थे वो एक याद बन जाओ तुम।

ना भूल पाऊँगा मै तुझे कभी किसी भी हालत मै ये मेरा वादा रहा।

तुम जीना मुझमै इतना की प्यार कम ना हो जाए मै रहु तुम से दूर
फिर भी

मै जी पाऊँ।

लिख कर दीवारों पर तेरा नाम एंक तस्वीर बनाऊँ उससे देख कर तेरी
याद मै कही शाहजहाँ ना बन जाऊँ।

छोटी सी उम्र मै एक वक़्त गुज़ारा है मेरी मौत की गुज़ारिश की हो तुमने ये इबादत करना उस रब से।

सफ़र के हर मोड़ पर करूँगा तेरा इंतेज़ार सुबह तक ।

तुम ज़रूर आना जो नही कहा मुझसे वो सब एक ख़त मै लिख लाना ।

उठा कर कलम लिखूँ उन पन्नो पर तो तुम किताब बन जाना।

ओर राही रहूँ मै तेरे सफ़र का मेरी जीवन संगनी बन जाना ।

ग़लत हम थे या तुम थे ये कुछ मत जानो।

लिपटे रहो हमसे करते रहो प्यार बस तुम इतना मानो।

सोचो क्या सोच होगी ओर जीत मिलेगी हमें किसी पड़ाव पर इतना तुम जानो।

जहाँ से की सफ़र की शुरुआत उसे अपना मंदिर मानो।

ओर उस मंदिर मै खुद को भगवान मत मानो।

तेरे इस जहाँ मै हर कोई बेगाना है यहाँ मानो तो पत्थर भी भगवान है ना मानो तो सब राख है।

डूब कर इश्क़ मै इतना फ़ना हो गया हु अब तुझसे मिलने की आस मै हर पल बेकार हो गया हु।

करते है हम बातें उनसे अपने दिलो की मगर ये बेक़ाबू भी तुम्हीं के लिए है ।

तुम आओ या ना आओ तुम्हारी याद आनी चाहिए।

जब धड़के ये मेरा दिल तो चेहरे पर मुस्कान आनी चाहिए।

जब बंद करता हु आँखे अपनी तेरा ही ख़्याल आता है।

मेरी कही हर बात मै ना जाने क्यों बार बार तेरा ही नाम आता है ।

मेरे इस दिल पर अब क़ाबू ना रहा ना चाहते हुए भी ये दीवाना हुआ।

ओर वक़्त के साथ प्यार के बहाव मै ये कब तुम्हारा हुआ ।

हम तो सोचते सोचते रह गये की कब ओर केसे बस तुम्हीं से प्यार हुआ।

कुछ तो सोचा होगा उस ख़ुदा ने मेरे लिए वरना इतनी भीड़ मै मेरे लिए वो तुझे ही क्यों चुनता।

हर एक पहलू का अपना नज़रिया होता है दिल मै धड़कन हो या
धड़कन मै दिल हो प्यार तो बस एक से होता है।
सुकून मिलता है जब मेरे दिल को जब तुमसे बात होती है ।
मुझे रहता है इंतेज़ार उन रातों का जब साल मै वो एक रात होती है।
एक रात होती है।

3

Akshata Hegde

Akshata Hegde is data science enthusiast and has co-authored more than fifteen books. She also blogs fictional

stories - Love Crush and Spook Tales. She also writes articles on spirituality and philosophy on her Facebook page- Sakhi. She loves to read and writing is her passion.

Love Beyond Borders

Two lovers distanced,
By miles of plain land,
Vast turquoise seas,
And a pandemic that gripped the world,
Restricting movements between continents,
And separating one
From their loved ones.

They were desperate,
Hopeless and terrible,
With painful separation,
Caused by this global issue,
And now regretting,
Chasing dreams over love,
And sacrificing watching
Serene sunsets at the lover's hilltop.

4

Aman Baghel

This is Aman baghel and he is 20 year old, is pursuing bachelors of commerce(B.COM). He live's in Selud, Durg, Chhattisgarh (INDIA). He like to write and indulged into it. He write his own diary too, and try to get ideas from every situations and feelings. He started writing one year ago.

Long distance

Long distance can't work
Guess we all heard it alot, and I know many of us do believe
this
I know that thoughts of losing your loved ones kills
but trust me after hearing it, will make you heal.
Being seperated from your loved ones is hard yet loving them
enough to let them go and trusting them with true intensions
will give your heart a bliss.
I don't know about Luck or Fate but i believe in intensions.
Energy of True intensions never fails, loving someone from
True intensions will always sets your heart ablaze forever
,even when you are apart from them.
Trust your true intensions for love and that never
disappoints.

5
Anubhuti Sachdeva

This is Anubhuti Sachdeva. Her native town is Basti Uttar Pradesh. She is persuading graduation from Bansthali university. She is 19 year old with hobby of writing. She was earlier part of 3 anthologies from quilling arena .

Connect to her with @kuch_lines_dil_ki

The distant time pass soon

Let's just hope
These times fly
Like butterfly in the sky

Let's just hope
The hardship won't long last
Prayers for distance to vanish fast

Let's just hope
These times will soon surpass
For life to be a pearl mass
After all life is an hour glass

Let's just hope
Negativity to blast
positive vibes and strength to be cast
And that we meet fast

6

Aparajita jha

Aprajita jha hails from Delhi, New Delhi. She completed studies from Sri satya sai vidya vihar and is pursuing Chartered Accountant along with Mcom from Delhi University. Writing was just a time pass earlier but then it became her passion.

Long distance relationship

The distance between us in Miles is nothing
Because Closeness of our soul makes everything,

You are not here for giving me a tight hug
But you are always there to hold me,

I know you are not here to make me smile when I'm sad
But you are there to charge me whenever I'm at my bad,

Since we were long apart,
I thought I was there in your darkened
But the distance made me that stuffy that we were shocken,

You wanted that shoulder besides you,who can hold you in my
absence
But this gradually changed my presence in my present,

But now, what we planned for the future is messing due to
your so called "coolness"
But my heart is forcing me towards darkness.

7
Ashi Sharma

This is Ashi, an ambitious writer who loves to write and express her jumbled collection of thoughts on pages which capture the depth of her musings into a steady flow of imagery.

She likes to portray the whirlwind of emotions with her jinxed pen, a dainty notebook and adequate amount of words, balancing the optimism in mind with the pessimism of the world.

Sacred flame

I remember the starry night, wind gusting giving me chills to the bone,
The flashbacks haunting me making my lips quiver while clutching your shirt which smelled faintly of your cologne.
I remember when we inscribed our names like counterfeit lovers on trees covered with pink leaves of blossom,
Now all I saw were the last lingering leaves crumbled up just like I did in your arms when I grew tired of my problems.
The tear- stained tissues and constantly rearranging my thoughts on pages comprehended loneliness while wading across a shallow stream,
But reading my notebook filled with musings of our love made me smile even in my whimsical dreams.
I reminisced about the days we ran into the obscure woods high on adrenaline under the radiant crimson moon,
When we encapsulated our promises in the jar of fireflies gleaming in the wild summer nights of June.
Now the distance has grown quelling the magnificent light from my heart by maiming it and infesting the rhythm of my heart beat echoes,
But you bandage my heart, blanketing it in the glow of green just like the glint in your eyes and with your sacred halo.
I remember when you adorned my neck with necklace engraved with a 'forever and a day',
Taking an oath that neither the gods above nor the devils who despise could engulf us in the bitterness letting the silver our love fade away.
-ashi

8
Ashima Mishra

Though a law student, I am also a literature lover since school days. Be it poetry or story, I imagine and create my own set of pieces. Poetry is something that gives me peace and stories motivates me to imagine!! I love to amalgamate my

thoughts and imagination in a piece of paper.

We Loved From Distance

It wasn't one sided,
We felt it together.
It wasn't only mine,
It was ours.
We chose to be together,
But destiny played its part.
We were broken together,
We were miles apart,
He departed,
I was deserted.
Only we knew,
How many scars,
Paved it's way!
We were supposed to be together,
We were segregated from each other,
We stayed miles apart from each other,
Love abridged our relation forever,
Disguising love as friendship,
We always did that to love our love!!
One of us worshipped Ram
And the other read namaz day and night!
Neither barrier of nations,
Nor country differences,
Created hindrances in our amalgamation!
She was in love with a man,
Who was fighting his own battles in the border,
He was in love with a woman,
Who was fighting with a world full of religious riots!

They needed no sanction,
To accept each other's emotion.
When they were together,
Their lives revived.
Thorns of separation haunted them,
They pined to embrace each other,
They yearned to walk hand in hand,
She felt his presence,
While wearing his fragrance.
He felt her,
By holding her scarf!
They chased the moon,
To find their moon.
Moon was the only mediator,
Which worked for the beloved and the lover!!

When she cried, he pined.
When he got injured, she felt the pain!
Their love was beyond every barrier,
Even though they weren't together!!

9

Avinash singh

Avinash singh
Silent, calm and composed..
An aspiring writer and a professional optometrist,
Lover of food,books and poetry..
Always carry a pen and a booklet to write.
Willing to be a content writer by end of 2021

Baat Dooriyon ki nahi..!

Baat Dooriyon ki nahi..!
Ki..
Baat Dooriyon ki nahi,
Door reh kar ye mohabbat aur badti jaa rahi hain...
Aur ye dil har pal tere liye ishq ka naya mukaam bana rahi
hain..

Durr rehna tum se bhale hi muskil hoo
Par tumse durr rehna mujhe tere aur kareeb lekar jaa rahi
hain..
Gumnam si meri iss Zindagi me tera Ishq apni pehchan
bana rahi hain..

Baat Pyaar ki nahi,
Pyaar mera har din ek naya sawera laa rahi hain..
Tujh se dur rehna mujhe Teri hone ki aasliyat bata rahi
hain..

Baat Riste ki nahi,
Rista mera Teri saaso se Banda hain..
Teri har saas meri Dil ki dhadkan bann kar dhadakti jaa
rahi hain...

Tera cehra Roz nahi dikhta mujhe
Teri baat Hal pal nahi sun pata hu main
Par palke Teri jhalak se duur nahi..
Teri har baat tasbir bann kar aankho ke saamne aati jaa
rahi hain

Tere Hone se meri pehchann bani hain..
Tere haato me meri taqdeer chupi hain..
Tera pyaar mere Zinda hone ka saboot hota jaa raha
hain...!

- Avinash singh

10

B. RAJI

B.Raji is from samayanallur(Madurai). At present she pursuing her first year of M.A.ENGLISH in english literature. She loves writing her memoir. Furthermore, with her ingenuity in the version. She has been a co-author author.

My Dearest

My dear after a long month , when I thought to meet up you,
met me
At an unexpected time we do not have
Long distance love my face suddenly
Becomes happy when I see something
In your memory on the way I go.
I pray to my favorite deity that you may
Come as my future life partner the
Desire to change long distance love and
Hold your hand with adult blessings
And live with you for a long time. It's my
Fantasies. Everything is future end......

11
Dhiman Sarkar

Enter Caption

Dhiman Sarkar is born and brought up in a small town named Moran of Assam. He completed his schooling from his hometown. Later he moved on to Dibrugarh for his high school and completed his graduation too. Presently he is pursuing his Post graduation. The very first novel he read was " I'm an average looking boy, Will you be my girlfriend?" by "Roopesh Kumar". He loves to write the genre Romance. According to Dhiman " Being Alone: Is a choice to stand in tough times".

Love Doesn't Comes With An Expiry Date

Its 5 in the afternoon at Pondicherry, Akhil entered Starbucks, pulled the chair and sat. Ordered a cup of Cappuccino and looked at the other tables. Suddenly, saw a couple entering the Starbucks. The girl was holding the hands of her boyfriend and he was looking passionately at her. She took Akhil's breath away and reminded him of his soulmate "Priyankshi".

Its been more than a year Akhil, met "Priyankshi". Everytime he saw a beautiful lady, he could see "Priyankshi" in his dreams staring at him angrily and getting jealous. Seeing the couple, Akhil missed her. Opening his gallery, he saw screenshots of their video calls. Scrolling the pictures he could see how silly they pose for the screenshots, suddenly he started smiling looking at the pictures and few drops rolled out from his eyes.

Completing the Cappuccino he left, and started walking towards "Rock bridge". On the way he saw couples enjoying the sea-shore and watching the sunset.

Looking at them Akhil smiled and started texting Priyankshi, "It's isn't easy to be in love with you and not being able to see you and hold your hands. Whenever I walk alone in the streets of Rock Bridge I, always feel incomplete, like some part of mine is missing. I know, presently this is how things are mend to be but its tough to bear the pain whenever I see other couples. You are far for my hands to hold, but too near to say: I LOVE YOU BABY. Everyday starts with your Good

Morning and ends with your late night video calls."
Few minutes later Priyankshi replied "I Love you too". Phone
rings Akhil recieved the call, it was Priyankshi. Priyankshi
asked him "Why do you love me so much?" Akhil replied
"There is no reason, no calculation and no question I just
Love you, after seeing your eyes, I haven't seen anything."
Lastly Akhil said "Love doesn't comes with an Expiry Date,
One day I'm goanna wake up, find you beside me and kiss
your lips and watch you smiling between our kiss. Whenever
I look into your eyes I felt like Home."
"Falling in Love with you is the best thing I did till date"-
Priyankshi.

12
Harminder kaur

इनका नाम हरमिंदर कौर है। ये जालंधर शहर पंजाब की रहने वाली हैं। इन्हे लिखना और पेंटिंग करना अच्छा लगता है। सादगी मे रहना पसंद करती हैं। इन्होंने M.com, MSc. IT, M.C.A और B. ed भी की है। ये कहती हैं की कुछ रिश्ते पास होकर भी साथ नहीं लगते और कुछ रिश्ते दूर होकर भी दिल के काफ़ी करीब महसूस होते हैं। ये Insta handle :- harart78 par quotes भी लिखती रहती हैं।

हवा का झोंका

बात आपकी करूं तो
हवा का झोंका है प्यारा सा
ये स्पर्श कर गुजर जाता है

मोल-तोल हो नहीं सकता
हर बार दिल क्या चाहता है
बिन-बोले कुछ भी
बहुत कुछ कह जाता है
हवा का झोंका है प्यारा सा
ये स्पर्श कर गुजर जाता है

आपमें सजग-सहज जो भीतर है
ये ख्याल जेहन पर मेरे छा जाता है
आपके किरदार का हिस्सा
जाने मुझे भी कहीं बहका जाता है
हवा का झोंका है प्यारा सा
ये स्पर्श कर गुजर जाता है

आपके ख्याल मे मेरा
कहीं तो नाम आता होगा
कभी - कभी जी अपना कहना
सब आपका बन जाता है
हवा का झोंका है प्यारा सा
ये स्पर्श कर गुजर जाता है !!!!

*****हरminder*****

13

Ishika Agrawal

Ishika Agrawal born and brought up in Atarra a small town in Uttar Pradesh she is passionate about her career taking up her writings at the same time she has been co- author of more than 15 anthologies you can follow her on Instagram, her Instagram I'd is @poetic_wish

14
Ishita Garg

Ishita garg she is a CMA student from Ghaziabad . She is good dancer and motivator . She love to write poetries and shayris . She believe to spread positivity and happiness around her

तूझे अपने पास पाती हूं

जब खुद से हार जाती हूँ, तुझे अपने पास पाती हूँ ।

इक पल ना लगा तुझे अपने क़रीब लाने में

ना जाने क्यूं तेरी ओर खींची चली जाती हूँ ।

जब तु हँसता है, मेरे अरमान पूरे हो जाते हैं

और जब तु रोता है, मैं पतझड़ सी विरान हो जाती हूँ ।

तेरे हाथ मेरे हाथ में और मेरे हाथ तेरे हाथ में

अपने हर कदम पे तुझे हमसफर पाती हूँ ।

बहोत शिकायत है मुझे ख़ुद से

पर तु हमेशा मुझे संभाल लेता है

क्यूँ है तुझे मुझसे इतना प्यार

कड़वी बातें कर जब तेरा दिल दुखाती हूँ।

कोई और होता तो कबका छोड़ चला जाता

फिर क्या खास है तुझमें ?

जो मेरी हर माफ़ी का हक़दार तुझे ही पाती हूँ।

मेरी राहें तेरी राहों से अब जुदा नहीं

कुछ सपने तु मेरे बुन ले और तेरे सपने मैं सजाती हूँ।

तु साथ है तो हर जंग जीत लूंगी मैं

हमारा मिलना अब और दूर नहीं मेरी जान

कांधे पर तेरा सर और हाथों में हाथ लिये बहोत दूर तलक चली जाती हूँ।

जब खुद से हार जाती हूँ, तुझे अपने पास पाती हूँ।

15
Ishwarya

Ishwarya is currently a first-year academy student. She loves to travel and explore new things. She began writing just now in this anthology. She found serenity in writing.

Email: ishwaryaihwarya2300@gmail.com

Unity of Love

*Only when the bird's extensions are divided, it will fly in the
sky
waiting as that will only increase the desire between the two.*

*Making love from duration is so adorable. when the two souls
are together the distance does not appear enormous when we
are far away do we know how much we adore one another.*

*There is no need for love that is touching or love that is with
fingers; enough love that seems to think of you all day
because the heart is melting even though it is far away.*

*Even if you are far away, your memories alone are enough for
me to survive in this world.*

*When someone is near us we do not know his awesomeness
Only when duration does realize how much we love Him.
Valentine compelled us to blush with memories not only if he
was near us but also far away.*

16
Kajal Singh

मैं, काजल सिंह,
महमूदाबाद,जिला सीतापुर, उत्तर प्रदेश की रहने वाली हूं।मैं एक प्रशिक्षु

अध्यापिका हूं।मुझे संगीत , डांस और कविताएं - कहानियां लिखना बहुत पसंद है।अलग अलग लेखन कार्यक्रमों में भाग लेकर अपनी बात लोगों तक पहुंचाना बहुत अच्छा तरीका है जनता से जुड़े रहने का।इस कार्यक्रम के साथ जुड़कर बहुत अच्छा लग रहा है।

प्यार वाली दोस्ती

"नहीं यार मैं नहीं मान सकती। हम तो बेस्ट फ्रेंड्स है ना, फिर क्यों हम अपने रिश्ते को कोई अलग नाम देकर उसको खराब करें।"उसने कहा। "पर यार हम दोनो एक दूसरे को समझते हैं। साथ में खुश रहते हैं, लड़ाई करते हैं फिर भी मना लेते हैं,तो अगर हम प्यार में हैं तो क्या बुराई है।"लड़के ने समझाते हुए कहा।लड़का काफी दिनों तक लड़की को मानता रहा उनके रिश्ते को प्यार का नाम देने के लिए । क्यों की दोनो को ही पता था की अब वो एक दूसरे को पसंद करने लगें हैं।बहुत सोचने के बाद लड़की ने कहा की ठीक है पर मैं एक ही कंडीशन में हां कहूंगी,"तुमको मेरे घर आना पड़ेगा मेरी फैमिली से हमारे रिश्ते की बात करने। क्यों कि मैं अपने घर वालों के खिलाफ कभी नहीं जाऊंगी। इसीलिए अगर तुम ये कर सकते हो तो ठीक है मैं हमारे रिश्ते को प्यार का नाम दे दूंगी।"

हां ,ये वही बेस्ट फ्रेंड्स है जिनकी मुलाकात एक सोशल नेटवर्किंग साइट पर हुई थी और अपनी 15 महीनों की दोस्ती मैं भी आज तक सामने से मिलना नहीं हुआ। दोनो की दोस्ती को शुरुआत 2020 न्यु ईयर पर हुई थी ।पूरा पिछला साल बहुत उतार - चढ़ाव भरा रहा,पर उनकी दोस्ती हर मुश्किल के बाद थोड़ी और गहरी होती चली गई। दूसरा साल आते - आते दोनों को एहसास हो गया की वो प्यार करने लगें हैं एक दूसरे से। हालांकि लड़की नहीं चाहती थी उनके रिश्ते को को और नाम दिया जाए वो तो बस उस दोस्ती के रिश्ते में ही बहुत खुश थी,पर लड़के से नहीं रहा गया तो उसने बोल ही दिया,"यार आ जाओ ना मेरी जिंदगी में मेरी हमसफर बनकर।जो इंसान मेरी दोस्त होकर इतना ख्याल रख सकती है वो प्यार बन जाए तो क्या गलत है? लड़की बस इसीलिए नहीं आना चाहती थी प्यार में आना क्यों कि वो अपने दोस्त को खोना नहीं चाहती थी।लेकिन फिर उसने अपने सबसे अच्छे दोस्त पर भरोसा करके एक नई शुरुआत का फैसला कर लिया।

दोनों ने तय किया की पहले अपना कैरियर बनाएंगे फिर अपने घरवालों से बात करेंगे । क्योंकि बिना सही कैरियर के कोई भविष्य नहीं है।बस वो दोनो इस नए रिश्ते को दिल से निभा रहे हैं,बिना एक दूसरे से मिले ।इस लॉन्ग डिस्टेंस रिलेशनशिप में भले 2 साल तक मुलाकात ना हुई हो,पर दोनों के प्यार पर कोई फर्क नहीं पड़ा है और दोनों साथ में खुश है।साथ ही अपने अच्छे फ्यूचर के लिए मेहनत भी कर रहें हैं, जिससे उनके घरवालों को ज्यादा प्रोब्लम ना हो उनके रिश्ते से।......

17
Khusboo Agarwal

Khusboo Agarwal,she is a student and a passionate writer with great ambitions. Every writings of her is based on true feelings and emotions. Though she writes a lot but she can't say that she is expert in writing. There are many more experiences to go. As a writer she have a lot of patience.

Long Distance Relationship

I really appreciate the couple who don't even get chance to hug,
They are so far that they can't even share coffee in the same mug..!!

The base of their relationships are only their trust,
They crave to see their partner other than the lust..!!

Long distance couples have a life with great fantasy,
Controlling this feeling is really not courtesy..!!

The happiness of surprising the partner with a surprise visit,
And again parting from them feels like shit..!!

The feeling of possessiveness and insecurity which kills,
But meeting them after ages feels like thrills..!!

Just because they are in a different zone,
It doesn't mean to them that you are none..!!

The only thing matters to be together is whom you prioritize,
And try balancing the relationship without any criticize..!!

18

Lakshay Agarwal

A nocturnal who likes to scribble, Lakshay Agarwal, hails from Ghaziabad, Uttar Pradesh. He is a Graduate from Delhi University. He occasionally writes his Thoughts and Feelings, which are at times good and relatable to readers.

मोहब्बत की कहानी

मेरी मोहब्बत की कहानी कुछ ऐसी देखि गयी
जैसे काटकर गाना ..... मूवी देखि गयी

उसे छोरडने पर, फिर इन आँखों में यारों,
बिन मौसम के .....बरसात देखि गयी

भला कैसे छुपता अपने ग़मों का राज़ मैं
मेरे चेहरे से पहले..... मेरी आँख देखि गयी

करता कोशिश तोह बच भी जाता मई मगर
मेरी नस टटोलकर थोड़ा देर से देखि गयी

मेरी मोहब्बत की कहानी कुछ ऐसी देखि गयी
जैसे काटकर गाना ..... मूवी देखि गयी

ज़िंदा थे तो तरसते थे मिलने को यारों,
बाद मरने के हर रोज़ हमारी तस्तीर देखि गयी

मेरी मोहब्बत की कहानी कुछ ऐसी देखि गयी
जैसे काटकर गाना ..... मूवी देखि गयी

मैं बताने से डरता हूँ

बहुत कुछ है पर मैं बताने से डरता हूँ,
मैं गुज़रे हुए उस ज़माने से डरता हूँ।

बहोत कुछ है जो जलता है अब,
आग जो लगी दिखाने से डरता हूँ।

निकल जायेगा मेरा दम इक रोज़,
क्या है वजह ये बताने से डरता हूँ।

जीने से पहले हैं ये मरने की आरज़ू,
क्यूँ है आख़िर समझाने से डरता हूँ।

दोज़ख़ में बीते लम्हों की सौग़ात,
कतरों से हैं सब दिखाने से डरता हूँ।

यूं न पूछा करो मेरे होने का सबब,
बेबुनियाद क़िस्सा सुनाने से डरता हूँ।

इतनी पीता हूँ कि मदहोश रहता हूँ,
सब कुछ समझता हूँ पर बताने से डरता हूँ।

आंसुओ से पलके भी कभी कभी भिगा लेता हूँ,
याद तेरी आती तो है पर दिखाने से डरता हूं।

सोचा तो कई बार है की भुला दु तुझे मगर,
लेकिन पता नही क्यों भुलाने से भी डरता हूं।

बहुत कुछ हैं पर मैं बताने से डरता हूँ,
मैं गुज़रे हुए उस ज़माने से डरता हूँ.!!

19

Megha Shapui is a simple college student studying Biology majors. She is an introvert who speaks through her pen. For her love is something you don't say, but you feel. She believes in happily ever after even if you are imperfect because love needs to be pure not perfect. She writes whatever her heart urges to express. A piece of paper and a pen are blessing to her.

It's Just Few Lightyears

It was late night when I looked at you. I smiled looking at you, well at the sky. I know you know that I miss you. After all we are so far away.

Few days ago it was your hostel and my room over a video call. Now you are few lightyears away from my balcony. You are over there and I am here. Nights passed away, but our Anatomy or Quantum Mechanics talk never came back.

I was once a girl who used to cry while watching Peter Parker losing Gwen, but never knew I would lose you.

I bid you goodbye for the last time and you took your leave once again. But this time you didn't leave your house or me, you left for forever.

Since the school ended we parted away with our colleges. Though my love never changed, definitely my fate changed. The school love became long distance relationship as you stayed in hostel away from me. But now the distance between two states changed into few lightyears.

Ever since our relationship became long distance one, I urged to see you more. But today under the open sky I stare at you believing that the brightest star is you just like everyone says. Now it's officially the longest distance relationship. Hope we meet again over there in heaven and in our next birth.

People say you are always with me. But how I wish to tell them you will be always with me as long as I live. But this heart never wants to understand. It craves for you since it started beating for you.

I accepted it as my fate, my destiny. One day this distance between us will end and we will be together, forever and ever.

After all it's just few lightyears.

20
Mili Kumari

Mili Kumari a most spectacular soul. Am a literature lover and pursuing Pharmacy.
Am in love with myself and love to grow self love.
Never hate your haters , it's my funda atleast they feel envy and what makes you the like

"Famous हो गई मैं।"

दूरियां

इन बातों को दूरियां,
हालातों की दूरियां,
ये जिस्मों की दूरियां,
ये सड़कों की दूरियां।
हम साथ नहीं,
पर तुम्हारी आवाज तो है,
ये दिल के जज़बात ,
तुम्हारा मेरे लिए प्यार,
मेरे सांसों का एहसाह,
न कम कर सकता दूरियां।
क्योंकि पास लाती है,
हमे ये दूरियां।

21
Monalisa Naik

Monalisa Naik, also known as @tale.of.heart._ , is a writer. From Bhubaneswar, Odisha, the city of temples. Started writing at a young age and was a co-author of "Kindred Spirits", "The Unprized" and many more. She is someone who enjoys making things and connecting with the universe.

She learnt to pay attention to her own requirements. To take it easy to keep going; to be patient; to persevere; to trust in her dreams.

"Wish You Were Here"

I look up at the stars,
And think of you tonight.
So I might,
Count every star to
Where you are.
And write you metaphors,
In millions with all the skies.
But really,
You just need to know.
I miss you.
I still have never
Seen stars like,
The ones in your eyes.
Wishing I could see,
Their reflection
In your eyes.
How I long to touch you,
Hold your body
Close to mine.
As we share our love,
Together beneath
The perfect sky.

22
Navya

She is Navya. She is a HR Executive by profession, A Writer, Poetess, Blogger, Podcaster by Passion. An Extrovert by heart ,An Introvert by Circumstances. She is also the

Founder of Merakians, Co founder of Spread Those Inks, Words of Wisdom . She is the Compiler of Stories from the Country Side, and a Co author of around 20 plus Anthos.

Long distance relationship

When she Unboxes the Gifts he sends .
Her Hapiness and Joy are infinite .
And Her smile is enough for him to be happy ..
Such is the happiness found in a long distance relationship..
Cherish these small things ,cause you live only once .

23
Navya Kapoor

Navya Kapoor is your typical teenager who finds it hard to express her opinions and thus annotates her thoughts on paper when she dreads eloquence.Through this micro-tale,she yearns to describe a vicious long distance relationship that every couple has to be in when one of them expires..

A destination beyond our love

"I am sorry to say your husband couldn't pull through the myocardial infarction"

3 years later....

"I reckon your love in the sun rays that light up the verandah and beam at the Dahlinovas that we planted in the green house;but oh my precious! My puny heart can't withstand until the extremity!"

24
Neelaksh Ojha

Neelaksh Ojha hails from Lucknow, Uttar Pradesh. He has

completed his B.com from Jai Narayan pg college and is pursuing Chartered Accountant. He usually writes as a part of his hobby. He express himself beautifully and love to write on different occasions . He always tries to bring smiles to everyone face.. He is always hopeful and bring positive memories to others .

The Most beautiful person : My love

Words simply can't describe
My feelings for you,
For my feelings are so many
But words, they are so few.

Hey you yes you ...The girl ...
U came into my life,
Like spring season..
With you I feel like
I have all the joy of the world...
We're far apart from each other ♥,
But u r always in my heart
The moon the sun act as our messenger..
Carry our message to each other
O my life I know
You are also watching the moon
This beautiful dark night as I am

You give your love so much,
As all the deep ocean of the world
Appears small in front of that...
Uttermost care and affection..!!
At last I just wanted to say that
You are my best friend my buddy..
And I had spent some of beautiful moments
Of my life with you.....

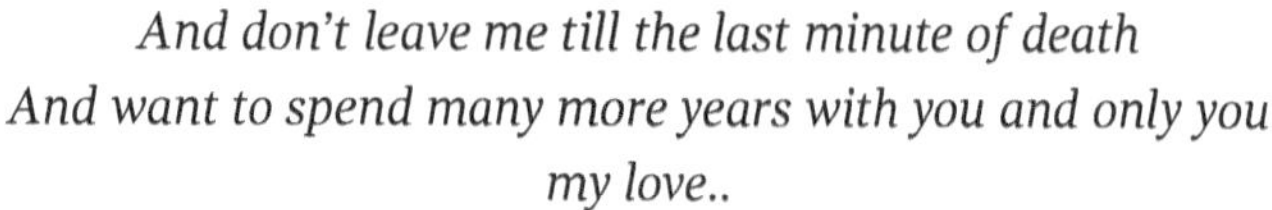

And don't leave me till the last minute of death
And want to spend many more years with you and only you
my love..
U r my heart for this life as I want to live with u die with you
....
Thanks for making my life such a beautiful song....

25
Nishchay Gola

My name is Nishchay Gola. I am from delhi. I am a student.

लंबी दूरी के रिश्ते

दूर होकर भी हम इतने पास है,
यही तो इस रिश्ते में ख़ास है।
मिलते रहेंगे यूं ही ज़िंदगी के हर मोड़ पर,
जब तक चल रही हमारी सांस है।

तुझे न देखने पर मन अक्सर होता उदास है,
फिर करते ही आँखे बंद होता मुझे तेरा अहसास है।
वैसे तो नहीं रहा जाता भूखा एक पल भी मुझसे,
पर तेरे साथ न लगती मुझे भूख और न लगती प्यास है।

कल देखे हुए एक सपने को पूरा करने की आस है,
देखना तेरे साथ राधा-कृष्ण का अदभुत रास है।
तुझसे मिले हुए हो गया समय इतना ज्यादा,
मानो जैसे सीता और राम का वनवास है।

इस रिश्ते की नींव केवल और केवल विश्वास है,
इसलिए नहीं करनी कभी चिंता और न होना हताश है।
दूर होकर भी हम इतने पास है,
यही तो इस रिश्ते में ख़ास है।

26
Piyush Maish

This is piyush masih, hailing vali poori line.
Piyush masih is pursuing his career as an Engineer in a MNC.
He has contributed in more than 5 anthologies as a coauthor and compiler of 3 anthologies in which one of them was awarded with India Book of Records.

दूर हूँ तुमसे

के दूर हूँ तुमसे और हूँ पास तुम्हारे,
मिल न सकूँ तुमसे, पर पा लूँ तुम्हे,
छू न सकूँ तुम्हे, पर छुअन न मिटा पाउं तुम्हारी,
यादों में रख तुम्हे, बिता लूँ ये ज़िंदगानी,

साथ न होकर भी, साथ हो तुम हमारे,
दूर हूँ तुमसे और हूँ पास तुम्हारे,
दुरी कितनी भी हो, पर दूर नहीं हूँ तुमसे,
दिन की शुरुआत हो तुम, और अंत हो तुमसे,
मेरी कहानी के एहम किरदार हो तुम,
मेरी हर ख़ुशी के हिस्सेदार हो तुम,
मेरी हर ख़ुशी के हिस्सेदार हो तुम ।।

27
Rakesh kumar

Rakesh kumar is from Buxar Bihar. Which is known as Viswamitra ki Tapobhumi. He is currently working in ICICI Bank. He likes to write poetry and quotes

चले आओ

चले आओ
अब हमें इतना
ना सताओ
तुम्हारे बिन
ये जिंदगी नहीं कटती
ये इक इक पल
बेचैनी सी हैं बितती
तुम चली आती तो
जिंदगी में बहार आ जाता
खट्टे पड़े
रिश्तों में भी
खुशियों का बहार आ जाता
ये जिंदगी भी
बड़ी नादान हैं
जो अपने रिश्तों की
जान हैं
हम दूर हों के
आज परेशान हैं
इस जीवन की
इक ही चाह अब ना
हों रिश्तो में
गैरों की परवाह
बस अपना और तुम्हारा
हों बस साथ

28
Riya Chauhan

Greetings of the day . Riya Chauhan is a 14 years old girl . She is currently in 9th Standard studying in Mayoor School noida . She was born on 8 February 2007 . Her hobbies are reading , writing , playing , with her little sisters and spending time with her family . Her mom ,her little sister and her family are the one's whom she love the most in the world . From her childhood till now she had a very precious dream and that dream is of becoming a teacher . She wants to fulfil her dream and achieve great heights in her life . She is really working very

hard to achieve what she wants in my life . At the end she would just like to say that if we are confident of our abilities and we believe in our self then we can achieve whatever we want in our life . Be strong and do great .

Thank You .

True Love

What is Love ? Love is a feeling of strong or constant affection for a person . Along with love people in this world have relationships in which love exists between two people but from a long distance . Love from distance is basically when two people are attached to each other by their heart but they are not able to meet each other . Once there was a young girl named Harini . She was 19 years old . she was tall , handsome and had long beautiful hair . She was very intelligent . It was the time when corona virus was spreading throughout the world dreadfully .All her studies were going on online . Once she got a message from a stranger through whatsapp . He asked him that " would you like to participate in an event "?. She asked for details and after reading the details , she agreed to attend that event . the boy who reached her with that event his name was Abhishek . He himself was also a participant in that event .So now they both talked to each other frequently through whatsapp . As time passed , they both became very good friends of each other . Now slowly and slightly Harini developed a liking for Abhishek . But she never confessed her feelings to him and the reason for it was that she was very scared . She thought that if she expresses her feeling to that boy then he will break their friendship also and will never talk to her because she thought Abhishek does not love her and for him she was just a good friend not more than that . Now Harini being very tensed took out her phone from her pocket and she tried messaging Abhishek . She just asked him that " How are you ? and what are you doing " . Then he replied answering her questions .

She felt a bit relaxed after receiving his message .but then again that thought of their relationship came in her mind . Which was now troubling her more and she broke into tears . A day passed . Next day in the morning she made her mind that " Whatever it is today I will express my feelings " and with a lot of courage she texted Abhishek that " I like you a lot and I Iove you " . After 4-5 hours abhishek replied . He texted " Harini what are you saying, I can't believe it , I thought that first I will express my feelings to you but I was scared that whether you also felt the same for me or not . " Oh my god really today's day is an auspicious day for me " . After reading the whole text Harini was on cloud nine . She replied " I just hope it's not a dream . Really I am now feeling that I really did a right thing after expressing my feelings , if I wouldn't have then we both would have been waiting for each other's message. So like this the relationship of Harini and Abhishek started . This short story depicts that how true relationships can exist even after being away from each other but having strong feelings for each other . According to me a strong friendship , trust on each other and true love can create a good relationship despite of having a long distance from each other . Distance is just a test to see how far love can travel . Waiting is a sign of true love and patience . Anyone can say I love you but not everyone can wait and prove it's true .

Thank you

29
Roshni Chaudhuri

The poem portrays the arrival of the poet from distance
when he found that his lover
Didn't loved him then. The poet even emphasized on his love
that made her go and him to move on

Hard to let it go!!

The Glory I saw when I went up to your doorstep,
The Resilient agony I figured when I caught you under my
breath,
Made me realise the love I was expecting was not there mine,
It had started belonging to an unco when I confide.
My eyes witnessed your change of Smile,
The touching sense has found its own menace,
I felt may be it was distance which was making me feel this,
But I sought to endeavour it was my love that helped me
making
you leave!!

I Hope You get!!

May be I was there all along,
The path we crossed by,
The songs we sang aside,
The cold that we took care of each other,
The night we had our heart broken to hide.
May be I was stupid enough to doubt you,
Each time you were with your friends and I swear I cannot undo,
For the last time I came to say you bye,
As it's too tough for me even to say you good-bye.
You will be given warmth in times of cold,
Joy in times of deep scars which cannot be healed alone,
But I hope you get that kind of love that you desired when we were two bodies One soul!!

Love is hard to be expressed!

It was October break. The sky full of clouds and it was the period of festivities all around. I remember as much as I could, It was night time with sparkling lights on, everybody in gorgeous dresses and that included me too. I saw my only friend in the crowd waving at me with a bright smile. I was new at that place headed a few minutes from my home so I got introduced with some new friends there. That's where I first met you. With a black short on, on with your hero hair. I can retaliat that situation now after almost 6 yrs, how embarrassed was I. Now, we are paths aside hardly get ahold of each other. I realised from that first day, this is going to be a trouble for me, loved you hard even knowing You weren't belonged to me!!

30
Rupsha Mitra

Rupsha Mitra is from Kolkata. She is in college pursuing her bachelor degree in Computer Science. Writing is her passion and she always finds a way to connect to her readers through her writings.

Letter from somewhere under the sky

To the one who lives miles and miles away from me,

While I am writing this short letter of love to you, I can feel you right by my side. Distance is bad but I believe that is not going to change the thing I have for you. I know you are figuring out the purpose of your life there and I am back here, finding ways to love you more. People say, this relation won't work out but this isn't the truth. We have true love and trust for each other. Isn't that enough? I know we will survive through this. I am ready to climb any highs and slip down through the deepest lows. I won't let you go even if everything feels worthless.

I miss our walk under the clear sky. I miss holding your hands and resting my head on your shoulder. This is a terrible feeling but somewhere deep inside my heart I have this belief that this terrible feeling will lead to the most beautiful bonding one day. The day we will meet, we will get everything like before. Live your dream. You will always have the way back to me- your home.

From
You know who

31
Sanskriti Basu

Sanskriti Basu is an aspiring writer who has been writing for 3 years. She has completed her post-graduation from Utkal University and has been a teacher since then. But her true passion lies in writing. She believes writing can elevate one's soul to the levels of enlightenment.

Something Named Love

I stopped replying to your texts once I realized it was nothing,
but futile.
I realized we no longer shared the love, that we shared years
ago while vowing our loyalty to each other.
I realized that this real distance between us had created a
massive void in our hearts, that no endeavour could ever fill.
And then, I realized more that this distance was present even
when we shared space.
I regretted our hearts drifting apart.
I mourned the absence of warmth, that I once felt in my
heart.
"We still care for each other!
Isn't that love?" screamed out Heart, in an attempt to
preserve whatever was left of love.
Brain retorted coldly,
"No, it is just a habit, that has arisen out of humanity.
It is no longer something, that once was named LOVE."

32

Sanya Bajaj

I am Sanya Bajaj.I belong from Faridabad, Haryana and is pursuing my Post Graduation from Jims, Kalkaji New Delhi also leading a NGO namely "Kind Beings". I am glad to be provided with an opportunity and platform to present my writings, for me it is neither a profession nor a hobby it was just beads of words which I used to tie in a tread to make a necklace out of it every morning and here I present one. I hope

you all like it and I get encouraged enough to work more in this field. Thank you so much.

ये सफर ह मेरा,
इस सफर का हमसफ़र हो तुम

ये ज़िन्दगी ह मेरी,
जिसकी मंज़िल हो तुम

तुम भरोसा हो, तुम ही फक्र हो मेरा

तुम एक किस्सा नहीं, तुम एक हिस्सा हो मेरा

ये तो रंग कई थे हमारे, पर भिन तम्हारे बेरंग लगते थे सारे

ये तो कश्ती थे हम, और किनारे तुम हमारे

मना हम खफा रहा करते थे, पर तुमने कभी वफ़ा न ठुकराई मौका तो
तुम्हारे पास भी था मुखर जाने का, पर तुमसे कभी बेवफाई न हो पाई

तुम मर्ज़ हो , तुम फ़र्ज़ हो , मेरी खुशियों पर एक क़र्ज़ हो

तुम साज़ हो, मुस्कराहट का एक राज़ हो
तुम ऐतमाद हो और तुम ही गुमान हो मेरा
मैं एक लम्बी रात हु और तुम मेरा सवेरा

ये सफर ह मेरा,
और इसमें हमसफ़र, तू मेरा!

33
Shivansh sharma

He is Shivansh Sharma. Basically, from Indore but perusing MBA(Marketing &Hr) in Mysore Karnataka. He always has a passion for writing the thoughts which come into his mind. A hardcore foodie as he belongs to Indore. He is the one who is always ready to help his near ones. His life revolves around his family and friends. He is always self-motivated, enthusiastic and a person with positive vibes. He is a co-author of 70+ books and a compiler of 4 book. currently holding the position of Ink Over Tears group Admin in Flairs and Glairs. His only belief is just to live happily and enjoy every moment of life. You can contact him on ig@shivanshrockzzzzz

long distance relationship

Too many hands to hold,
Yet I search for the best,
The one that gives me butterflies,
The one that knows my happiness and sadness just by
hearing your HELLO..!
Someone too far yet so near,
How good is it ..?
If the world would be like shelves of books and the pages may
get changed without separation and forever togetherness..!
Wandering around the library,
Moving around the world with you in your arms,
Reading gave me this pleasure,
Smilingly were the pages who saw me in my fairytale
You went soo far,
Yet I could feel your presence all near,
The relationship was just always alive,
The one that was just soo pure,
Because the time you gave me was little though,
But the memories are just so fresh in my head,
Just too when I feel low,
I just keep my hand on my heart,
Because when you left,
You just said in my ears,
Sooner or later
Will be holding you just closer..!

34

Shubhashish Ranjan

शुभाशीष रंजन {SR36} बिहार के एक छोटे से शहर जमालपुर के रहने वाले एक नवोदित लेखक हैं। वह वर्तमान में दिल्ली विश्वविद्यालय के क्लस्टर इनोवेशन सेंटर से स्नातक की पढ़ाई कर रहे हैं। उनका मानना है कि लेखन एक टूटा हुआ दिल ठीक कर सकता है, और दूसरों को जीवन में आगे बढ़ने के लिए प्रेरित कर सकता है। वह लगातार ऐसा करके अपने पाठकों को प्रेरित करने का प्रयास करते हैं। वह कई गैर सरकारी संगठनों और प्रकाशनों से भी जुड़े हैं क्योंकि ये उनकी रुचि के क्षेत्र में आते हैं।

आप INSTAGRAM I. D. @ranjanshubhashish और YourQuote I. D. SHUBHASHISH RANJAN पर उनकी कुछ रचनाये पढ़ सकते हैं।

आप उनसे उनके ई-मेल के माध्यम से भी संपर्क कर सकते हैं : shubashishranjan36@gmail.com

ख़ास एहसास

वो एहसास थी,बहुत ही ख़ास!
हमारा वो रात तक वीडियो कॉल करना,
और कहीं पकड़े न जाए,इसके लिए डरना!

बातें करते करते ना जाने कब सो जाते थे ?
सवेरे जब उठते तोह खुदको मोबाइल से चिपके पाते थे¡
एक दूसरे से मिले बिना भी इतने पास हो जाते है !
लोगो के बीच रहकर भी, आप उनमे ही खो जाते है !
दूर रहकर भी एक दूसरे पर विश्वास करना !
रिश्ता टूटने की बातों से भी न डरना |
हर कुछ दिनों में एक दूसरे का रूठना मनाना,
कॉल पर बात के लिए घर से बहाना बनाना|
छोटी छोटी गलतियों के लिए बार बार डांटना ¡
हर सुख दुःख के पल एक दूसरे से बांटना |

इन्ही चीज़ों से तो हो जाता है मजबुत आपका प्यार ¡
सच्ची, लॉन्ग डिस्टेंस रिलेशनशिप बेस्ट होती है यार |

35
Sourabh Vishwakarma

Nirbhik Lekhak is a pen name, he started writing 4-5 years back, but after his brekup during covid-19 lockdown he started writing seriously. He is a storyteller, writer, listener and a photographer.

"तुझसे पूछूंगा में"

मैं हूँ यहां, तू कहीं और है।

सुना है ये इश्क़ की डोर होती कमज़ोर है।

ये इश्क़ के दरिया में, दुरियों का सैलाब कैसा है,

ये झील सी तेरी आँखों में, पानी कैसा है,

तेरी मोहब्बत में, ये दिन-रात कैसा है,

आवाज में तेरे ये, अफसोस कैसा है,

जो फोटो तूने भेजी, वही हसता चेहरा अच्छा है,

विडियो कॉल में ये, मायूस चेहरा कैसा है,

आज फिर नेटवर्क का ये, मसला कैसा है,

तेरी-मेरी दुरियों का, ये सिलसिला कैसा है,

तेरी बातों में ये, कैसा नशा सा है,

तेरे लबों के जाम का स्वाद कैसा सा है,

तेरे होठों से ज्यादा मोबाइल को मैंने चूमा है,

हर कॉल में तेरी सांसों को भी बड़ी ध्यान से मैंने सूना है।

हर रात होती यही बात है की कब मिलेंगे हम!

वो एक पल जब हम मिलेंगे , तुझसे पूछूंगा में "हाय, ये मंज़र कैसा है"।

36

Sreeparna Ghosh

She is Sreeparna Ghosh, a 3rd year student of BSc in Media Science from Techno India Salt Lake, Kolkata. She is from Durgapur and she passed her 10th and 12th from St. Michael's School durgapur. She is a very energetic and jolly person. She loves meeting new people and create memories. She is a very

sports enthusiast person. Photographer by passion and film maker and youtuber by profession. She loves music and creativity and that's what developed her hobby for hawaiian guitar and dance. She believes that the best way to utilize one's life is to help people in need and that's the reason she is doing Rotaract for the past 3 years being the Director of Public Relations for Rotaract Club of Calcutta Lansdowne. Whenever she feels that she needs someone to express her feelings that's when she picks up her pen and paper and writes.

Her moto in life is -

"Zindagi ek hai aur achieve karne ke liye Pura jahan."

तुझसे दूरी अब सही जाए ना

तुझसे दूरी अब सही जाए ना
तेरे करीब जाना है
तुझे बाहों में लेके तेरे बालो को सहलाना है
ये दर्द अब सही जाए ना
तुझे गले लगाके
सारे गिले सिकवे दूर करना है
तेरे कांधे पे सर रखके
तुझसे बातें करनी हैं
मुझे फिर से मुस्कुराना है
जो तेरे चेहरे को देखके आता था
मुझे वो मेरी मुस्कान चाहिए
मुझे तुझे महसूस करना है
तुझे चुन्ना है तेरे आँखों में खोना है
तुझसे ये दूरी अब सही जाए ना
तुझसे दूर अभी रहा जाए ना

37
Sruthi

Sruthi is a 20 year old with many dreams and passions. She's so passionate about writing and tries her best to express herself through her write ups. Apart from her beautiful write ups, she also has a soulful voice so reach out to

stuffi_wannasay on all social media platforms.

The Wait

Starting my day with your good morning
As it curves my lips upwards.
I text back to you waking
and remembering our good old days.

Back when you were with me,
When a second of parting hurts.
I wondered how I'd manage
It's still not easy to do this.

I facetime you as I get ready,
Having our breakfast together and leaving
As the whole work gets heady,
Only your words are soothing.

When will I see you, honey?
To hold you in my hands, I yearn.
Asking the same question daily,
Waiting for you to return.

38
Sunil Maheshwari

सुनील माहेश्वरी एक मोटीवेशनल लेखक, विचारक, कवि, प्रेरकवक्ता ,ब्लॉगर, शायर, और आर्टिस्ट, हैं, आपकी बहुत सारी कविताएं, लेख, राष्ट्रीय समाचार पत्रिकाओं, सोशल मीडिया एप, मैगजीन, और ई पत्रिका में प्रकाशित हो चुके हैं, और पंच प्रवाह, कलम और ख्याल, सैटायटी, संघर्ष, कहकशां के सह लेखक भी हैं। साहित्य

रचना सम्मान पत्र से सम्मानित किया गये हैं। हिंदी लेखन, मोम्सप्रेस्सो, स्टोरी मिरर, साहित्य रचना, कोरा एप, शंब्दांचल, मिराकी, में बहुत से लेख, आलेख, कविताएं प्रकाशित और सम्मानित हो चुकी हैं, और आइकोनिक पर्सनेलिटी ऑफ द ईयर के प्रशंसा पत्र से नवाजे गये हैं।

"क्या यही प्यार है"

काँटो वाली राह में,
किसी के गुलाब बन जाना,
किसी के ग़म में शरीक होकर
यारों उसका मन लुभाना,
किसी की संवेदना को,
दिल से सहानुभूति जताना।
किसी के रोते हुए चेहरे की,
खिलखिलाती मुस्कान बन जाना।
किसी के आहत मन को,
एक सुकून भर देना,
किसी की ग़लतियों पर,
आहिस्ता से समझा देना।
तो कभी ग़लती पर,
उसके गुस्सा दिखा देना।
कभी खामोशी से उसके,
लफ्ज़ पढ़ लेना।
तो कभी खाली किताब में,
एक शायरी लिख देना।
कभी डांट में छिपे,
अहसास की पहचान,
कभी बारिश में भीगते,
पंछियों की शान,
कभी ख़्वाब में तराशे,
ठिकाने बनके,
कभी अल्हड़ मस्ती के,
अफ़साने बनके,

कभी मासूम सूरत के,
दीवाने बन के।
प्यार को बखूबी,
समझा जा सकता है जनाब।
ये प्यार की बातें हैं,
जहाँ दो नफरते भी,
जिंदादिल मुहब्बत,
बन जाते है।
जो मर कर भी शान से,
एक दूजे का साथ निभाते हैं।

39

Surbhi Vishwakarma

यह जो कविता लिखती है;
वह खुदको सुरभी कहती है;
बस चाहती है इतना कर पाय;
किसी का दिन सुरभित हो जाय!!

तुम कब आओगे!

चेहरे-चेहरे इतने सारे;
पर सारों में बस कुछ ही प्यारे;
उन प्यारों में जो सबसे प्यारा;
क्यों उसका ही दूर ठिकाना ;

हाय !ये कैसी व्याथा हो गई ;
मीलों दूर ये आंख खो गई;
पल दो पल की ही मुलकात में ;
चैन छिन गया रात छिन गई;

जाने शहर तेरे गयी ही क्यों ;
गई भी तो तुझसे मिली मैं क्यों;
मिलकर फिर जो ये हाल हुआ है;
एक दिन एक साल हुआ है;

इन लंबे लंबे सालो में ;
कुछ एक दो दफा ही आए हो ;
तो,आगे क्या विचार हुआ है ;
बोलो! कब ये साल घटाओगे?
तुम मुझसे मिलने कब आओगे?

40

Tania Sarkar

She is Tania Sarkar. She resides in kolkata. She is a teacher. She likes to scribble and her hobby is reading. She has a dream to live in the mountains.

Love during Partition

They knew Partition would happen soon,
His father would go
to India and her father would be in Bangladesh.
His father knew he had no way but go to India
But her father knew he
could not live anywhere
else other than his
ancestor's land.
They both were in love,
truly,madly and their love
knew no boundaries.
She knew he would be miles away from her as they would go
by the train which would go to India.
But she would wait.
May be,someday
he would return.
He thought,his love was eternal for her and when he would be
mature enough,he would be back to her by the same train.
No partition,nothing could stop him to do that.
There was an unconditional love between both. While he
would miss his birth place and his beloved so much,she would
miss him more and more as she would be all alone soon.

Now its almost 20 years,the partition happened.
She was doing some household works when she noticed a tall
man with sharp features was standing in front of her.
It took no time to recognise her love and she did not know
what to say because she was so happy as well as so surprised

41

Tarun batra

मैं तरुण कोटा राजस्थान से हूँ ।
एक सफर का राही हूँ , जो सफर में है उनको हसाना यही काम है अपुन

का ,
पागल हूँ थोड़ा पागलपन कर लेता हूँ ।

कुछ बातें

कुछ बातें है जनाब , उनको बातें ही रहने दो,
वो कुछ बातें ही जीने का मजा देती है ,
सफर में ही कुछ बातें हमारी है तो कुछ उनकी भी है,
जो सफर को अपना हमसफर बना देती है ,
शायद यही कुछ बातें है जो कुछ बातों से मिलकर बनी है,
कुछ मतलबी है , तो कुछ अपनी है , कुछ परायी है , कुछ किसी से
मिलकर है,
यही है जो जिंदगी की कुछ बातें है ।
चाहत रखु क्या किसी से ,
यही कुछ बातें है जो जीने का सलीका बताती है ,
यही कुछ बातें है जो जीने का मजा देती है ,
जनाब कुछ बातें है , उनको बातें ही रहने दो ।।

42
Tejaswi Pappu

Tejaswi.Pappu is born and brought up in vishakapatnam,andhrapradesh .it's ,the city of destiny always inspires her to be more creative and thoughtful.she completed

M.Tech. she is working as assistant professor in engineering college. She is a former educationist, Passionate writer, communication trainer ,Amateur of nature ,wanderlust and avid reader .she is a writer who shares her emotions and thoughts through words, which conveys message in amicable way.she is a coauthor for 150+ anthologies and has got pages

https://www.yourquote.in/trendytejaswi

https://www.facebook.com/trendytejaswi/

she wrote more than 500 quotes,which are inspiring and heart touching.she always feel 'writings is stress buster !'

Distrusted Trust Happened !

Should I live?
How could I, after you made me lost!

Should I breathe ?
How could I, after you smothered my feelings!

Should I dream?
How could I, after your absences became
nightmares!

Should I fly again?
How could I, after you destroyed the last feature of my dream
wings!

Should I love again?
How could I, just forget the special moments that spent!

Should I trust again?
How could I, just forgive the backstabbing moments that
caused!

43
नुसरत परवीन

मेरा नाम नुसरत परवीन है
मैं एक माध्यमिक परिवार से हू

मैं एक विद्यार्थि हू
मेरे पापा का नाम नौशाद आलम है तथा माता का नाम रुखसाना परवीन
है
मेरे पिताजी एक शिक्षक है,
मुझे लिखने की प्रेरणा मुझे अपने पापा से मिली इस रुचि को मैं आगे
लेकर जाऊँगी

दूरियां

चलो एक दुआ तो अपनी पूरी हुई
मिल लिए तुम अपने दीवाने से
करो कोशिश की हम तुम्हारे रहे
दूरियां बढ़ जाती है बढ़ाने से
सीढ़ियां उतरता सूरज
फलक पर चमकते पहले सितारे से
मुस्कराकर मिला होगा
जब तू मुझसे मिला होगा

कुच्छ इस तरह ज़माने को हम पर कायल रखेंगे
हम दूरियों मे भी इश्क को हमारे कायम रखेंगे
एक दूसरे के गलती से खफा भी होंगे
तो मिलकर एक दूसरे से रजा भी होंगे
हर वक़्त तुझे सीने से नहीं लगा पाऊँगी
लेकिन हर रात फोन पर करके बात मैं ही सुलाऊगी
बस किलोमिटर मे फर्क रहेगा
पर मुझे तेरी बेइंतहा इन्तेज़ार रहेगा

44

अंतरा चौधरी

अंतरा चौधरी, नागपुर महाराष्ट्र की निवासी हैं । वह पिछले कुछ सालों से लिख रही हैं। उन्हें लिखने का शौक हैं ।उन्हें भ्रमण करना भी

बहुत पसंद है । वह कहती हैं की जज़्बातों को लिखकर ज़ाहिर करने से दिल को सुकून मिलता हैं और लिखकर दिल की बात ज़ाहिर करना भी एक कला हैं। उन्हें पढ़ना और लिखना दोनों पसंद हैं । उन्होंने 50+ अन्थोलोजी एवं 1 डुओ किताब में काम किया है और 3 किताबें संकलन के तौर पर काम किया है और 4 किताब आने वाली है ।

वो खुद को खुशनसीब मानती हैं की वह बहुत ही सरल भाषा में लिखती हैं ताकि सब पढ़ सकें।

संपर्क करने हेतु -

इंस्टाग्राम - antarachoudhury.15

विश्वास : प्यार की डोर

इश्क़ तेरी आँखों में मैंने कुछ यूँ देखा,
लगा जैसे बरसों से तेरा ही इंतज़ार किया,

दिल की दुआ थी मेरी कोई अपना मिले
तुझे पाकर ज़िन्दगी मेरी रंगीन हुई ,

फिर एक वक़्त आया जब एक दूसरे से
हमें दूर जाना था पड़ा
मगर दूर जाकर भी पास होने का एहसास हुआ ,

दूर जाकर भी जब भरोसा तेरा पाया ,
लगा जैसे मैंने अपने अधूरे हिस्से से खुदा ने मिलवाया,

कांधे पर तेरे सर रखकर सुकून का एहसास जब किया,
यकीं मानों जीना का मतलब मैंने जाना,

हाथों में हाथ रखकर चलने का जब भी मन है करता ,
तेरी तस्वीर गले से लगाकर मैंने तुझे अपने करीब पाया,

हमारे प्यार के डोर का नाम है विश्वास,
यही है हमारे दूर होकर भी पास रहने की वजह,

बंधन है जो पक्का हमारा,
कभी टूट पाए ना ये रिश्ता हमारा ।।